Put Beginning Readers on the Right Track with
ALL ABOARD READING™

The All Aboard Reading series is especially designed for beginning readers. Written by noted authors and illustrated in full color, these are books that children really want to read—books to excite their imagination, expand their interests, make them laugh, and support their feelings. With fiction and nonfiction stories that are high interest and curriculum-related, All Aboard Reading books offer something for every young reader. And with four different reading levels, the All Aboard Reading series lets you choose which books are most appropriate for your children and their growing abilities.

Picture Readers
Picture Readers have super-simple texts, with many nouns appearing as rebus pictures. At the end of each book are 24 flash cards—on one side is a rebus picture; on the other side is the written-out word.

Station Stop 1
Station Stop 1 books are best for children who have just begun to read. Simple words and big type make these early reading experiences more comfortable. Picture clues help children to figure out the words on the page. Lots of repetition throughout the text helps children to predict the next word or phrase—an essential step in developing word recognition.

Station Stop 2
Station Stop 2 books are written specifically for children who are reading with help. Short sentences make it easier for early readers to understand what they are reading. Simple plots and simple dialogue help children with reading comprehension.

Station Stop 3
Station Stop 3 books are perfect for children who are reading alone. With longer text and harder words, these books appeal to children who have mastered basic reading skills. More complex stories captivate children who are ready for more challenging books.

In addition to All Aboard Reading books, look for All Aboard Math Readers™ (fiction stories that teach math concepts children are learning in school); All Aboard Science Readers™ (nonfiction books that explore the most fascinating science topics in age-appropriate language); All Aboard Poetry Readers™ (funny, rhyming poems for readers of all levels); and All Aboard Mystery Readers™ (puzzling tales where children piece together evidence with the characters).

All Aboard for happy reading!

For Adele—S.S.

GROSSET & DUNLAP
Published by the Penguin Group
Penguin Group (USA) Inc., 375 Hudson Street, New York, New York 10014, USA
Penguin Group (Canada), 90 Eglinton Avenue East, Suite 700,
Toronto, Ontario M4P 2Y3, Canada
(a division of Pearson Penguin Canada Inc.)
Penguin Books Ltd., 80 Strand, London WC2R 0RL, England
Penguin Group Ireland, 25 St. Stephen's Green, Dublin 2, Ireland
(a division of Penguin Books Ltd.)
Penguin Group (Australia), 250 Camberwell Road,
Camberwell, Victoria 3124, Australia
(a division of Pearson Australia Group Pty. Ltd.)
Penguin Books India Pvt. Ltd., 11 Community Centre, Panchsheel Park,
New Delhi—110 017, India
Penguin Group (NZ), 67 Apollo Drive, Rosedale, North Shore 0632, New Zealand
(a division of Pearson New Zealand Ltd.)
Penguin Books (South Africa) (Pty.) Ltd., 24 Sturdee Avenue,
Rosebank, Johannesburg 2196, South Africa

Penguin Books Ltd., Registered Offices:
80 Strand, London WC2R 0RL, England

Photo credits: cover photo: © AP Photo/Jason DeCrow; title page: © Joe Kohen/WireImage; page 4: © Getty Images, Getty Images; page 5: © AP Photo/Seth Wenig; page 7: © AP Photo/ Seth Wenig; page 8: © AP Photo/Jason DeCrow; page 9: © TIMOTHY A. CLARY/AFP/Getty Images; page 10: © Chris Hondros/Getty Images; page 11: © Chris McGrath/Getty Images, TIMOTHY A. CLARY/AFP/Getty Images; page 12: Seated Mastiff, c.100 (earthenware) by Eastern Han Dynasty Chinese School (25-220) ©Indianapolis Museum of Art, USA/Eleanor Evans Stout and Margaret Stout Gibbs Memorial Fund/in Memory of Wilbur D. Peat/The Bridgeman Art Library; page 13: Ostrich-feather fan from the Tomb of Tutankhamun (c.1370-1352 BC) New Kingdom (wood covered with sheet gold) by Egyptian 18th Dynasty (c.1567-1320 BC) ©Egyptian National Museum, Cairo, Egypt/The Bridgeman Art Library; page 14: © AP Photo/Daily Sentinel, Dean Humphrey; page 15: © AP Photo/David Foster, AP Photo/Keystone, Andree-Noelle Pot; pages 16-17: © Tim Graham/Getty Images; pages 18-19: © AP Photo/Seth Wenig; page 20: courtesy of Jim O'Connor; page 21: courtesy of Jim O'Connor; page 22: © AP Photo/Mark Lennihan; page 23: © AP Photo/Mark Lennihan; page 24: © AP Photo/Seth Wenig; page 25: © AP Photo/Amy Sancetta; pages 26-27: © AP Photo/Jason DeCrow; pages 28-29: © Chris McGrath/Getty Images; page 30: © AP Photo/Jason DeCrow; page 32: © Joe Kohen/Wire-Image; page 33: © AP Photo/Jason DeCrow; pages 34-35: © AP Photo/Richard Drew; page 36: courtesy of Scott Radachi/Charlie Rose; page 37: Bennett Raglin/WireImage; pages 38-39: © AP Photo/Frank Franklin II; page 41: © AP Photo/Jason DeCrow; page 43: © Joe Kohen/WireImage; pages 44-45: © David McNew/Getty Images; page 46: © Stephen Chernin/Getty Images; page 48: © AP Photo/Seth Wenig.

Library of Congress Cataloging-in-Publication Data is available.

ISBN 978-0-448-45073-5   10 9 8 7 6 5 4 3 2 1

Uno
Blue-Ribbon Beagle

By Stephanie Spinner
With photographs

Grosset & Dunlap

Beagles are great dogs.

They start out as

supercute puppies.

*A beagle puppy
at four weeks old*

A beagle puppy at three months old

As a puppy,

Uno was more than cute.

He was handsome and friendly

with round, golden-brown eyes.

His tail never stopped wagging.

He was special.

When he was only

eight months old,

Uno won top prize—

a blue ribbon—

at his very first dog show.

What made the judges

choose Uno?

Were Uno's eyes gentle

and pleading?

Was his chest broad?

Were his legs strong enough

for a long, long run?

Was he everything

a beagle should be?

The answer was—yes!

After his first show,

Uno went on to win hundreds

of blue ribbons.

Then, in 2008, his handler

Aaron Wilkerson entered Uno in

the Westminster Kennel Club Dog Show.

It is held every year
in New York City.
It is the most famous dog show
in the world.
In 2008, 2,627 dogs competed.

There were 169 different breeds.

Breeds are like dog families—

groups of dogs that

look and act the same.

Cocker spaniels are one breed.

Great Danes are another.

And then there are toy poodles.

They are hard to miss.

Some breeds are very, very old.

There were mastiffs

in ancient China,

guarding the emperors.

Hounds hunted
with the pharoahs
of ancient Egypt.

Each breed has

its own special talents.

Border collies herd sheep.

Huskies and malamutes pull sleds.

Saint Bernards

rescue people.

Beagles hunt.

When they're on the chase,

they howl.

(It's called "baying.")

Beagles bay to call hunters

and other dogs in the pack.

Beagles also bay when they're really excited. Some show dogs are quiet and serious. But not Uno! Uno liked to bay at dog shows. It was like saying, "Hey, you guys! I LOVE doing this!" Beagles also make wonderful pets. They are very good with young children.

Many dogs are a mix of breeds.

They make wonderful pets, too.

But mixed breeds

do not compete in dog shows.

In 2007, Uno was

the top-ranking hound

in the country.

But no beagle had ever won

the Westminster Kennel Club Dog Show.

That honor usually went

to a less common breed.

In 1999, it was a papillon.

In 1988, it was a Pomeranian.

In 2001, it was a bichon frise.

In 2008, Westminster was full

of amazing-looking dogs.

One by one,

their trainers took them around the ring.

Dogs at Westminster

work hard.

Sometimes all a dog needs

is a nice, long nap.

The finalists for
Best in Show
were all champions:
an Akita,
an Australian shepherd,
a Sealyham terrier,
a standard poodle,
a toy poodle,
a Weimaraner . . .
and Uno!
Lots of people were
rooting for him.
Was there a chance
he could win?

He was up against
great dogs.
But the little beagle
wasn't worried.
He trotted around
the ring cheerfully.
Whenever the judge
looked his way, he bayed.

"He's a merry little hound,
and he was having a great time,"
said Aaron Wilkerson.
"All I had to do was hold
on to the leash and follow him.
He did the rest."

Whatever Uno did, it worked.

The judge paced

for a few minutes.

Then he called,

"May I have the beagle, please?"

That meant Uno had won!

He was the number-one dog,

and guess what!

His name means *one*

in Italian and Spanish!

Thousands of fans

leaped to their feet.

As the arena exploded with cheers,

Uno trotted up for his prize.

He bayed when he got it.

Uno was very busy after his big win.

He climbed inside his trophy.

He met reporters

and chewed on

their microphones.

Beagles are a very popular breed.
So people all over the country
wanted to learn more about Uno.

He went on lots of television shows.

Here he is with Aaron

on *The Today Show*.

He visited Charlie Rose

and Macy's department store.

He ate a big steak at a famous
New York City restaurant.
Everywhere Uno went,
Aaron went, too.
"I met him when he was
six months old," said Aaron.
"We've never been apart
a day since."

Aaron has been

a dog handler

since he was nine.

He was the Top Junior Handler

in the country

for three years.

Of all the dogs he's known,

he's closest to Uno.

Aaron said,

"Uno always had

a great attitude.

Dog shows were fun for him.

We always knew

he would be a winner."

Now that Uno has won

Best in Show

at Westminster,

he is retiring.

He'll have his toy frog

to play with.

Aaron and his wife

train many dogs.

So Uno will have lots of friends

for company.

After Westminster

he became a therapy dog.

Because Uno

just makes

people smile!

Therapy dogs
are trained
to visit hospitals
and nursing homes.
They come in
all shapes and sizes.
Therapy dogs
don't have
to be champions.

But they do have to be

friendly and loving.

Their job is to

cheer people up.

And guess what?

Uno is going to be

a therapy dog, too.

Uno will be a

great therapy dog.

Why?